V.G CAUSERANO

Audit Etiquette

Copyright © 2024 by V.G Causerano

All rights reserved. No part of this publication may be reproduced, stored or transmitted in any form or by any means, electronic, mechanical, photocopying, recording, scanning, or otherwise without written permission from the publisher. It is illegal to copy this book, post it to a website, or distribute it by any other means without permission.

First edition

This book was professionally typeset on Reedsy.
Find out more at reedsy.com

Contents

1 Audit Etiquette	1
Introduction	1
Auditors	2
List of Rules	4
The Rules Explained	4
Tell the truth - ALWAYS.	4
The Questions.	7
Experts answer questions.	9
There's no requirement to answer things FAST.	11
No one should speak with the auditors alone.	11
Show your gaps.	12
Never argue with the auditor.	13
Eat and Drink.	14
BREATHE.	14
The Checklist	15
2 Conclusion	16
Also by V.G Causerano	19

1

Audit Etiquette

Introduction

The auditors are coming, the auditors are coming.... sounds ominous, right?

Well, it doesn't have to...

But I know right now you are saying "there are so many things to be done, so many questions to be answered, so much to be aware of".... I know.

And you are right – there are – but first and foremost – relax!

People tend to get very stressed out when audits are forthcoming. We all spend time running around and trying to ensure everything is perfect. This can be very challenging and very difficult. And it is usually the least successful way to approach an audit.

The best way to prepare for an audit is just to do what you're supposed to do all year round.

Now, before you toss this book to the side and deem me an ass for pointing out the obvious – I realize that it is much easier said than done. My goal here is to help you prepare for your next Audit (which may be right around the corner) and to help you make sure the one after that is super smooth as well, so I hope you keep reading. (If you really want to figure out how to get and stay prepared all year round - check out my other book, *Blue Print for Quality* in the **QMS Blueprint Series** or call me, I will help).

Many times, a variety of tasks get in the way of doing what we know we should (and we will talk about *planning better* later), but for now, it becomes a matter of "what are we going to do when these auditors show up?". What if we're not perfect? What if we have things that are out of compliance? How are we going to handle that? How can we minimize damage?

We want to do well. Sometimes, there are severe consequences if we don't do well – consequences from our company or clients. All the thoughts flying around in our heads can be very concerning, distracting us and making us worry about what we're doing. So, we need to put those thoughts to rest and focus on the task in front of us.

Auditors

It is very likely you are going to be audited by humans (if this is not the case for any of you, please drop me an email so we can discuss). THEY ARE HUMAN – just like you and I. Some are tall, some short, some women, some men, some young, some older, some just old. My point is that we all fit into one or more of the above categorical descriptions. Your auditors are just like you and I. Auditing is their job. They get up every morning and want to perform their job well and have a good day at work. No one wakes up and says "I want to have a terrible day at work today!" and that goes for auditors too. A good day at work for auditors involves finding opportunities for improvement or areas with gaps to fill. Notice I didn't say "finding problems" or "catching people doing xyz". Like most humans, auditors have feelings and know that almost no one likes them when they visit. It's hard to walk into a company when you know everyone is counting the moments until you leave. A good auditor looks at their job as an opportunity to make the organization they are auditing better. They are looking for ways to recommend improvements and best practices to an already functioning infrastructure. I share this with you because I think people forget that auditors are people. I believe it is a good reminder every now and again because we have all had negative experiences with a person or two – and one or two negative experiences doesn't mean they will all be bad. Every auditor is different – they bring something different to your table. Instead of approaching him or her with fear or suspicion, try approaching with an open mind and see what you can learn from them. I promise, if you listen closely – you will learn a bunch.

I've sat in on hundreds of audits conducted by a multitude of agencies and groups, and I'm also an auditor and have conducted hundreds of audits on hundreds of companies. I look at every audit as an opportunity; I think if you approach it:

1. as an opportunity to have someone look at what you say that you do, and how you do it, and
2. as an opportunity to get feedback on what some other best practices might be or ways you can improve what you do.

It'll be a much better experience for you, the people you work for, and those that work for you.

List of Rules

1. Tell the Truth
2. The Questions
3. Only Experts Answer Questions
4. There is no requirement to answer questions FAST
5. No one is alone in the room
6. Show your Gaps
7. Never Argue
8. Daily Meetings
9. Eat and Drink
10. Breathe

The Rules Explained

First and foremost, there are some basic rules and guidelines you should abide by with an audit.

Tell the truth - ALWAYS.

You don't ever want to find yourself lying to an auditor. I have had multiple experiences where I have been in an audit as an observer and witnessed people lying in an audit. I can tell you that they get caught each and every time –and it always ends badly. If you position yourself as untrustworthy, any auditor will question everything you say. This is not a position you want to be in. You are far better off being upfront and transparent. Let them know where you think you have gaps or, if something isn't quite right, or even if you *think* it might not be quite right, but it's your best practice, stand by it and ask for advice. Say the truth no matter what it is. Let me tell you a story: I was with another auditor, and we were doing a site audit, and as part of it, we were touring the facility. One of the standards the facility needed to meet involved the data center and requiring that the room's walls be cement and go from floor to ceiling in an enclosed room so somebody can't just crawl over a drop ceiling. It is a straightforward thing to check and verify. All you have to do is look up under the ceiling panels and check. So we're doing a tour, and the employee representing the company gets to the data center. We thought he had been a little cheeky with us a bunch of times but figured it was no big deal —everybody's nervous. We're in *their* data center.

So I say to him, "Since you have your servers in here, do all of the walls go all the way up to the ceiling of the building?"

He said, "Oh yeah, absolutely."

I said, "Are you sure?"

He said, "Yeah, I am."

Then I said, "Okay." I was explaining to him the reason why this must be the case.

He was like, "Yeah, absolutely – it's the way it needs to be, blah, blah, blah."

I said, "Great." With that, I put down my tablet and the other stuff in my hand. I put my hands on one of the desks, and I pushed it over to the corner.

He said, "What are you doing?"

I said, "Well, I'm going to check."

He said, "Well, I just told you they do."

I said, "I understand. As an auditor, it's something I need to verify." I pushed the desk over, jumped up on the desk, popped out a ceiling tile and guess what? No cement wall. He was quiet after that. I was not happy. *We* were not happy. The thing is, if you're going to lie to me about that, something that can very easily be verified, what else are you not being honest about? Why would you lie about that? Take the observation. It's not like you'll get closed down because of a finding like that – take the recommendation, and then those things become negotiable. **Tell the truth.**

I have another example of a time when I was in an audit, it was one of my very first audits and again, I'm observing. The company is being audited by three foreign individuals, which seems to make everybody very nervous (which I thought was interesting). I don't know if it was the accents or if people just had difficulty understanding. But I am once again, in a data center. I don't know why this always happens in data centers, but I'm in the data center and the auditors are asking about the security recordings. The company volunteers that they have cameras that record what goes on in the data center around the clock. They are being questioned about the monitors and how often they watch the tapes and that sort of thing. The guy (representing the company) was going on, and on about how, yes, they monitor the recordings, they are made every day, and then transferred to VHS tapes, the tapes are watched, and they check the tapes every day. They watch them right there on the VCR, that's in the room with them.

So, the guys representing the company are talking to two auditors standing directly in front of them and are going on and on about how they just used that VCR to watch the recording. Now the third auditor had wandered behind the other two auditors with the plug to the VCR in his hands. The VCR plug is clearly not plugged, it's not near an extension cord, and it can't reach an outlet from where it is. One of the other auditors sees his compadre standing there swinging the plug, the guy talking can't obviously see this, and I'm having a stroke in the corner because it's very clear that he's lying, and they're going on and on.

He's like, "Do you watch the tapes every day?"

"Yes, we just put them right in, it's very simple."

"You use the VCR right there?"

"Yep, it's right there. It's connected to this television. It's what we use every day, blah, blah, blah."

"You used it today?"

"Yes, absolutely blah, blah, blah."

They go on and on. The next thing you know, the two auditors separate their stance so the third auditors standing there with the plug, and with his very thick Russian accent basically says, "Can you explain this?" Again, the guy falls silent.

Why lie? He could have absolutely said that the place is recorded all the time. He didn't have to go into the detail that they're watched every day, blah, blah, blah because that was clearly not true. You don't want to do that. He volunteered information that was utterly unnecessary and got caught in a gigantic lie. Now the three auditors are standing there wasting 15 minutes of their time telling stories, and you can bet now, they're just going to rip you from end to end trying to find out what's going on because clearly you are not being upfront.

Don't Lie: Be Transparent.

The Questions.

Answer only the questions you've been asked.

I'm sure you've watched T.V. shows of lawyers and courtrooms where they say, "Just answer the questions; don't elaborate." It's not quite that strict, but only answer questions you have been asked. You don't always need to elaborate; less is more in these circumstances.

Make sure they understand what you do.

When you're talking to the auditors about the final report, remember that they are HUMAN and can make errors. They may think they know exactly how you do things or they may have some idea, but the chances are good that they don't know all the specific details of what's happening in your world. You need to be cognizant and pay attention. Be sure to give them enough information to understand. Sometimes it's good to start with a question, confirming you understand what they are asking in the context of what you do. This will likely require information. Let's assume all you do is process claims, and somebody says, "Do you provide product information to the patients on the phone?" Well, that's kind of vague. Do you provide product information? What do you mean by product information? Do you mean information about a specific drug? Do you mean information about their benefits? Do you mean claim information?

You could say something like, "Regarding what we do on the phone, we only process claims, so the only information that I would be sharing would be information related to their claims." And stop there. Then they could follow up and ask, "Well, what if somebody asks you a question about a specific product?" Then you could respond with something like, "Well, when it comes to product questions, our standard operating procedure would be to..." and then say what you do if that happens. Very simply giving only the information necessary to make a clean, clear answer for the auditor. Those things are important again because you want to make sure they understand in the context of what you do. Many of these auditors audit many different types of businesses, manufacturing sites, call centers, fulfillment houses, and clinical trials. Regulations can be different across all sites so sometimes the auditor can get caught up in what they think the rules are. Sometimes it's helpful to point out to them what rules you follow. You can say things like, "We're following Training123, which is the training provided by the client and stipulated in our contract and statement of work. According to Training123, we are required to do x, y, z related to administration, and we follow our client approved standard operating procedures which states blah, blah, blah." Let your experts speak to your processes – do not speculate or say what you "think" is right. You need to know what you are talking about. Which is why we have rule number 3.

Experts answer questions.

Make sure the expert on the topic is talking to the auditor. If the questions are IT related, the IT people should be in the room. If it is an operational question, the Operations folks need to be in the room. If it is a question about your quality standards, your QA people need to be in the room. While it is very likely that many folks share cross-knowledge, it becomes cumbersome and depletes confidence when one person must correct the answer of another person on the same team. Auditors are trained to respond to what they see and hear and to read between the lines. If an operational person answers a question about quality processes and that answer is incorrect and subsequently gets corrected by the quality experts – confidence in the operational person immediately drops. As an auditor, I would absolutely press the ops person more, about all sorts of other areas so see if I can identify any other gaps or deficiencies. The theory is if there is one level of misunderstanding – there is bound to be more – and remember, it is the auditors job to find these areas so if you give them a little hole, they will likely investigate it. And truthfully, the operational person may just be misinformed because it is not their area of expertise - it doesn't actually mean that anything is wrong- but it can create a whirlwind of digging that is really unnecessary. If some gets asked a question in an area where they are NOT the expert – it is perfectly acceptable to indicate that and get the expert. For example, if my expertise is call center operations and somebody asks me a question about fulfillment processes, I should not be answering the question. I should appropriately respond, "We do have someone in charge of fulfillment processes and I would be happy to arrange for you to speak with him/her directly". If you think this statement will be difficult to make, practice it until it is comfortable.

Schedule people. It's entirely acceptable to work directly with the auditors to schedule the interviews. It is very likely that the auditors will give you an audit plan. If they do not, ask them for one. It can be very basic, such as on day one we are going to review all documentation. On day two in the morning, we would like a facility tour followed by interviews for the rest of the day. And so on and so forth. When they mention the interviews, ask them if they know who they would like to speak to first, second, etc. They understand that you have a business to run and that it may not make complete sense to have everyone in the room for hours, unless of course, it is appropriate to the discussion or to the staff. If your team is especially nervous, then it may be helpful to have them in the room so that they can see what is actually happening, and perhaps not be quite as anxious. I still get nervous in audits regardless of if I am the auditor or the auditee— it's just the nature of being human. So do what you can to put people at ease, but ultimately you want to protect the staff and their time.

There's no requirement to answer things FAST.

If an auditor asks you a question, and again, you're not the best person to answer it, you can say something like, "That's not a task I complete every day, let me get you the person that does that." You can take down the question and say, "Okay, do you have any additional questions about this topic so we can gather a team of people more properly fit to deliver quality responses?" This can allow you the time to provide a thoughtful answer. Now there will be times where it will look kind of odd to do that, and you can give an answer without delay, but it needs to be a thoughtful answer because you want it to be appropriate. What you don't want to do is say something that's clearly out of line that opens you up to other questions. The object is to not feel the need to rush an answer AND to provide the most complete AND correct answer possible.

No one should speak with the auditors alone.

A convenient way to make sure that doesn't happen is to assign a notetaker. This is a person whose entire function of the audit is to keep notes of the questions asked, answers given, observations mentioned, requests made, items delivered and anything else that happens. They should not be answering questions. It is actually very helpful if they are in a position *not to have to answer* any questions -meaning this person could be someone outside of the audit – so they can keep a consistent focus. This sounds simple, but it is a hard role. They need to stay focused during what can be boring or confusing conversations. There may be multiple conversations happening at once that need to be summarized and recorded. Additionally, when people enter and leave the room, they should "check in" with the notetaker to make sure he or she has the person's name and position correct. The Audit leader or coordinator for the company should be meeting with this notetaker often to make sure that questions are being answered and requested deliverables are being provided. The audit coordinator will also want to be sure that notes are accurately reflecting what is happening in the room. These notes will be very helpful if there are any discrepancies of understanding. One of the most important functions this notetaker has is to note when an auditor points out a gap or an observation while reviewing information. If you can manage to get that observation corrected before the end of the audit, many times they will not put that information in the final audit report or if they do, it's written as closed. That is a great thing. The more credit you have for the completed work, the better you are.

Show your gaps.

There will absolutely be times when you have a practice or a procedure that you know is not effective, not efficient, or not the best it could be. When this is the case, your best effort may be to be completely transparent about this issue. When the topic or question comes up, you may want to lead with that. You may want to say, "Yes, I know that you guys are looking at this. It's been a place that we've struggled to have something that we can successfully follow and manage. We realize there are gaps in it. Any input that you may have, or recommendations to help us to understand how we can fix this, or implement any best practices, we would very much appreciate." By being transparent, it shows that you have insight. Auditors want to know that YOU know what is going on in your organization. Do YOU have an awareness of the problems that your company is facing? Insight helps dramatically – companies with no insight have FUNDAMENTAL problems - huge gaps, huge problems, no quality control, systemic issues – because they are not watching, not listening. They don't want to learn. They try to argue their way out. Those are companies with problems. You don't want to be one of those companies; you want to be knowledgeable. You want to be involved. You want the auditor to know that YOU know what's happening; that's a real benefit. Don't be afraid to share those pain points when you see them. Don't be afraid to ask for help. Don't be afraid to say, "Hey, yes this is definitely an issue. It's something we're struggling with. It's something we've tried multiple solutions for. Here's what we've tried and each time, we fall a little bit short." That is entirely and wholly acceptable, and, it will be welcomed. I would suggest thinking about what items fall into that category before the audit and be prepared to look at those.

Never argue with the auditor.

If you're getting to a point where you feel like you're having a misunderstanding that you can't get resolved, it may be best to have somebody else do it; especially if you're getting frustrated. Take it off-line; have everyone get some space and get some perspective, and then re-approach the situation. Arguing will not resolve anything.

1. Daily Meetings.
2. Have a morning meeting with your staff BEFORE the auditors arrive. Check in with everyone; see how things are going. Are there open issues or problems that you know are going to arise? Be prepared to address any issues.
3. Have daily close out meetings with the auditors – if they agree. Discuss any open items or questions, next steps/the next day's agenda, or any other items that they may need.
4. Have a daily close out meeting with your staff AFTER the auditor close out meeting. This will allow you to assign any open tasks,

answer any questions and make sure you are prepared for the next day. All these meetings might seem like overkill. I promise you they will be helpful. Some will be lengthy – most will be brief. They will be worth it.

Eat and Drink.

I know it sounds simple and I know it sounds kind of silly, but we are not at our best when we're hungry. Our blood sugar drop, and we're not as sharp or as tolerant as we can or should be. Make sure your auditors are fed and hydrated. It is nice to have food available for them – not only for meals but for snacks as well. Absolutely address this issue ahead of time, with the auditors. Let them know you'll be providing breakfast, lunch, snacks, and drinks for them, if they intend on having full working sessions. If there's an issue with that, they'll let you know. And don't forget to check for any allergies or restrictions – it's just nice to do. Obviously, you're not going to take your auditors out for dinner. That is frowned upon, but you can offer them a meal that is provided onsite with other people. That will keep them refreshed. Do the same for your people; you need to make sure you stay, again, fed and hydrated because this is stressful. Audits are challenging. Audits – even at their very best, still feel stressful.

BREATHE.

Just remember to breathe. When things get tense, tough, scary, nerve-wracking – take a moment, stand up, step into the hall, and take three slow deep breaths. It will clear your head and recenter you. Approach every audit as an opportunity for growth- a way to make your next day better than the previous day. You can do this.

The Checklist

- **Be Honest always**
- **Explain what you do well**
- **Answer only what has been asked**
- **Experts answer questions**
- **Take the time you need to get the correct answer**
- **Don't leave anyone alone with the Auditors**
- **Show gaps - again BE HONEST**
- **Do not argue**
- **Keep everyone fed and hydrated**
- **Breathe**

2

Conclusion

Following these steps will help you know you are doing it right. Every audit should teach you something new, pay attention and be sure to debrief afterward with all of your people:

- what went really well?
- where were the pain points?
- what was a complete disaster? (hopefully nothing :-))
- what felt good vs. bad?
- how can we improve?

Once you have these questions answered, update your checklist for the next audit.

Sometimes, the approach I suggest you take (*everyone looking for opportunities to improve*) is NOT the culture of the organization being audited. Sometimes their are other approaches organizations like to take:

- the **"daze and confuse"** approach - this is where the company throws

CONCLUSION

so much information at the auditors in the hope that they are not able to make sense of anything and just give up. It can be in the form of lengthy or numerous documents that have many words but low level content or by using leadership members to talk incessantly about things that do not follow any logical pattern
- the *"yes you to death"* approach - this is where the organization says YES to everything an auditor could possibly ask and then is never able to produce an validation or proof of anything actually existing
- or the *"nope, can't have that"* organization - this is where the organization hides behind "its proprietary" for every answer and is not the least bit transparent.

Some organizations - are really good at blending all three of these tactics as well . There are two points I would like to make about these types of places:

1) **Auditors know immediately**. These tactics are **instantaneously** identifiable. And any auditor that has faced these tactics will have no trouble navigating the situation and making appropriate recommendations. The tactics do not help. The auditor s job is find areas for improvement. Approaching with these tactics lets an auditor know immediately that their job is going to be easy.

2) If you find yourself working for a company that operates like this, I would urge you- **go get a different job**. Organizations that look to hide, confuse, misrepresent, or outright lie are destined for failure. It is a cultural issue that runs much deeper than having a good Quality and Compliance team and effort. My guess is if you are looking for tips on how to make your audit more successful, you have more integrity than to lie and cheat your way through - find a culture that matches YOUR integrity. Notice that "integrity" contains the word GRIT. GRIT is not

a word that is used very often any more. As a psychological construct GRIT is a positive term that combines the ideas of perseverance and passion as it relates to a goal. It is defined as a firmness of mind or spirit : unyielding courage in the face of hardship or danger. As a Quality professional you MUST have GRIT. Everyday you will need to stand tall in what is right and true - each and every time. You will need to do it when it feels good and it is easy, when it is hard and requires more explanation, and then it is in direct opposition to what you are being asked to do. And if you are in an environment that does not embrace the true meaning of Quality Improvement and Compliance, and does not provide the support necessary to spread this culture, no amount of GRIT is going to help you maintain your sanity. (I know you wont compromise your integrity - you have worked too hard!).

I wish you much success in every audit. Should you have any questions, please don't hesitate to contact me. I can be reached via my webpage at vgcsolutions.org or find me on LinkedIn.

If you found this book helpful, please leave a review on Amazon.com and look for other books in the QMS Blueprint series.

Thank you and good luck.

Also by V.G Causerano

BLUEPRINT FOR QUALITY
A super simple but robust plan to help you implement a complete Quality Management System with ease.

DISASTER RECOVERY BUSINESS CONTINUITY IMPLEMENTATION
A clear and foolproof methodology to implementing small and large scale Disaster Recovery and Business Continuity plans without getting completely overwhelmed.

www.ingramcontent.com/pod-product-compliance
Lightning Source LLC
Chambersburg PA
CBHW071003220526
45471CB00007B/3149